Living Your Baptism in Lent

Weekly Reflections for Your Journey

Dennis Strach, csc

LTP

LITURGY
TRAINING
PUBLICATIONS

Nihil Obstat
Rev. Mr. Daniel G. Welter, JD
Chancellor
Archdiocese of Chicago
September 17, 2019

Imprimatur
Most Rev. Ronald A. Hicks
Vicar General
Archdiocese of Chicago
September 17, 2019

The *Nihil Obstat* and *Imprimatur* are declarations that the material is free from doctrinal or moral error, and thus is granted permission to publish in accordance with c. 827. No legal responsibility is assumed by the grant of this permission. No implication is contained herein that those who have granted the *Nihil Obstat* and *Imprimatur* agree with the content, opinions, or statements expressed.

LIVING YOUR BAPTISM IN LENT: WEEKLY REFLECTIONS FOR YOUR JOURNEY © 2020 Archdiocese of Chicago: Liturgy Training Publications, 3949 South Racine Avenue, Chicago, IL 60609; 800-933-1800; fax: 800-933-7094; email: orders@ltp.org; website: www.LTP.org. All rights reserved.

This book was edited by Christina N. Condyles. Víctor R. Pérez was the production editor, Juan Alberto Castillo was the designer, and Kari Nicholls was the production artist. Art direction by Anna Manhart.

Cover art and interior part art © Marianne Scheel. Interior line art by Martin Erspamer, OSB.

24 23 22 21 20   1 2 3 4 5

Printed in Canada

ISBN 978-1-61671-516-8

ELBL

CONTENTS

INTRODUCTION

My first assignment as a newly ordained priest was at St. Ignatius Martyr Catholic Church in the Diocese of Austin, Texas. If you were to walk into our parish on Ash Wednesday, you might think it was Easter Sunday or Christmas Eve. The pews were completely packed for each of the five liturgies that were celebrated on that first day of the season of Lent. There is something momentous about the annual reception of a cross of ashes. It goes beyond a simple external sign and speaks to the profound yearning of our hearts. These ashes are an outward symbol of penance. They are a reminder of both our mortality and our desire to turn away from sin and be faithful to the Gospel. And yet, this desire can never be satisfied through our actions alone. The soul's yearning reminds us that it is God who is transforming us. He is drawing us ever deeper into the salvation offered by Christ's cross. This external sign of victory traced in blessed ash is a sign of our complete dependence on God and our need to surrender ourselves to his grace and mercy. Bearing the cross of Christ, our communal witness speaks boldly of our collective yearning for a lasting, transformative, and healing encounter with the living God, whose Holy Spirit changes us.

Before we were ever marked with ashes, we were marked with the Lord's cross at our Baptism. Indeed, we are baptized in the name of the Father, Son, and Holy Spirit. These words recall our identity as people who have been adopted as sons and daughters by the Father through Christ and in the power of the Holy Spirit. It is no accident that the ashes are sprinkled with holy water before we receive them. The season of Lent is not just a time for us to work on *our* Lenten plan, through prayer, fasting, and almsgiving. It is also a time to become more profoundly aware of *God*'s plan for us that began with our Baptism. The goal of all our Lenten actions (and the entirety of our Christian life) is to keep God's saving work at the forefront of our minds, so that our words and deeds lead others to know God and seek him with all their heart.

For many of us who were baptized as infants, the sacrament of Baptism can become something that is only recalled when we walk through the doors of our churches and bless ourselves with holy water. Baptism can become a sacrament of the past, a sort of "one and done" celebration that does not have much of an impact on our daily lives as Catholics. This Lenten season, however, brings into our midst the elect, those men and women who are responding to the voice of the Lord by preparing to become Catholic through sacraments of initiation. As they prepare to receive the sacraments of Baptism, Confirmation, and the Eucharist at the Easter Vigil, we, the Church, walk with them. And while they look to us for a witness of what it means to bear the name of Christ, we look to them as well. We see in their longing for God our own continuing thirst for a deeper relationship with God. As they reject sin and profess their faith in Christ Jesus, we recall the same vows made at our own Baptism and recommit to that life of discipleship and mission. As they journey toward Easter and new life in Christ, we accompany them by conforming our lives to Christ's life. Lent helps us to see our Baptism as the unending work of becoming children of God and the ongoing hope of conversion according to the will of the Spirit.

How to Use This Book

This reflection book will help you to be open to God's transformative power throughout your Lenten journey. In the first three weeks of Lent, **Part I: Turn Away from Sin** reminds us that in order to have a relationship with God, we must continually work to reject the influences of sin and evil in our lives. During the final three weeks of Lent, **Part II: Turn toward God** recalls our belief in the Triune God and his continual presence in the world and in our Church. **Part III: Living the Baptismal Life** invites us to continue deepening our relationship with God throughout Easter Time and beyond, striving to always live as witnesses of Christ's saving work.

During Lent, each week's reflection recalls one of the questions asked before Baptism. These questions are also used when we, the baptized, renew our baptismal promises at the Easter Vigil or on Easter Sunday. Each week's reflection helps us to understand what it means to say "I do" to the question at this moment in our lives (🜢 Baptized in Christ). After setting up the question and its role in our lives, we are then called to deepen our awareness of the way we share our faith with others

(✠ Witnesses of Faith). Each week's reflection concludes with questions for personal reflection and suggested Scripture readings (📖 Praying through the Week).

For those interested in using this book with small faith sharing groups in a parish, with family members, or friends, please visit https: //ltp.org/products/details/ELBL to download the **Leader's Guide for Small Groups** that can be found by clicking on the "Supplement" tab. This free guide will help you lead sessions by providing an outline for each week, including prayers and group discussion questions.

About the Author

Rev. Dennis Strach, CSC, was ordained a priest of the Congregation of Holy Cross in 2016. Prior to his ordination, he earned a bachelor of music from Oakland University. He also earned a master of divinity from the University of Notre Dame, where his research interests included sacramental theology and the missionary activity of the Church. As parochial vicar of St. Ignatius Martyr Catholic Church in Austin, Texas, Fr. Strach was involved in preaching and teaching on the sacraments and in Hispanic ministry. He currently serves as associate director of vocations for the United States Province of Priests and Brothers. Fr. Strach is from Rochester Hills, Michigan.

About the Artist

Marianne Scheel is a Denmark-based illustrator with an Argentine twist. When she was five years old, her family moved to Argentina to live on her grandfather's farm. This close contact with the wonders of nature proved to be the perfect spot for a child to cultivate her creativity. As a teen, she fell in love with the art form of illustration upon discovering the natural beauty of the planet captured in a world atlas. After studying illustration, she studied graphic design and worked in that field for a number of years. In 2015, she returned to illustration and now focuses on creating handmade illustrations in watercolors or mixed media that work in harmony with a written story, capturing feelings, situations, and moods. Her website is www.mariannescheel.dk.

Part I: **Turn Away from Sin**

Our annual celebration of Lent, beginning on Ash Wednesday, encourages us to turn away from sin. In an attempt to rededicate ourselves to our Lord once more, Catholics examine the state of their relationships with God, others, and themselves through the lens of three spiritual disciplines: prayer, fasting, and almsgiving. We seek to answer this call to conversion (literally "turning" or "changing direction") through our actions. Typically, we will develop some sort of Lenten plan and resolve to give something up or to do something; perhaps the two are even related. For example, we might decide to give up an expensive coffee drink and donate the money we saved to a charitable cause. Whatever it is we decide, we must remember that these acts are a means to an end. The ultimate end of our Lenten journey is a deeper relationship with God. As we begin this journey, we should spend some time reflecting on the purpose of our actions. We are not setting out to impress God with our personal goals. In small acts of faithfulness and humble obedience, we are opening ourselves to God's will.

This Lenten theme of conversion is also an important part of our understanding of Baptism. Conversion is a lifelong process and Lent helps us to remember that. If the invitation of the season is to "turn away from sin," then the things we give up or take on are meant to turn us toward a more enduring life with Jesus that began with our Baptism. The catechumens, who have been discerning God's call over the past several months, are seeking to give their entire lives to Christ. Catechumens are those people who, by taking part in the Rite of Acceptance, have publicly declared their intention to participate in the sacraments of initiation. Their presence in our liturgies and throughout the world reminds us that Lent is about responding to the grace of Baptism, which is an eternal and life-sustaining gift from God. It was at Baptism where the minister first asked us to reject sin and profess our faith in Christ Jesus. If we were baptized as infants, our parents and godparents were asked these same things, accepting the responsibility to raise us according to that faith. Our baptismal identity calls us to continually renew our commitment to the God who first made a commitment, a covenant, with us and called us his own. Lent is a time to intentionally respond to God's call.

And yet, no matter what we have planned, it will not be enough to make us saints. In the midst of all of our planning to be holy, it is easy to forget that God has a plan for us too! As we make our concrete efforts to rid ourselves of sin, we are invited to consider the movement of the Holy Spirit already in us. This movement is happening right now, sustained by our ongoing participation in the sacraments. The works of holiness in our lives can only be accomplished through Jesus Christ, whose Paschal Mystery offers the grace of salvation to the entire world. Jesus was conceived, lived, died, rose from the dead, ascended to the Father, and sent his Spirit to animate us and dwell with us. This is his Paschal Mystery, the source of our salvation. Because of the victory of the cross, any aspect of our lives can speak to us of God's faithfulness: our triumphs, joys, sinfulness, and brokenness. Every cross comes with resurrection. Because of Christ's Paschal Mystery, the work of grace is being accomplished in us each and every day. Unfortunately, many times while we're busy trying to chip away at our own projects of holiness, God is silently revealing to us something of profound beauty, hope, and truth . . . and we don't even notice. Our works of repentance, prayer, fasting, and charity must be a means to an end, not the end in and of themselves. They invite us to hear God's voice, encounter his presence, and belong completely to him by accepting his grace.

In this first part of our Lenten journey, we will consider the Renunciation of Sin, the first three questions that are posed to those who are about to be baptized and to us when we renew our baptismal promises. We will consider our own Baptism in light of these questions and open ourselves to conversion.

WEEK 1

Do you reject sin so as to live in the freedom of God's children?

Rite of Christian Initiation of Adults, 238

 ## Baptized in Christ

At St. Ignatius Martyr Catholic School, Mass was celebrated every Friday morning. It was always a challenge for me to preach these Masses because the congregation included students ranging in age from three to fourteen years. That meant, of course, a lot of differing attention spans, family situations, and understandings of the faith. On occasion, during the homily I would ask the students questions to help them engage with the message of the readings. Admittedly, I would call on the older kids more often for these questions because I always felt bad telling the younger kids, "That's not the answer I'm looking for," when they would respond with a liturgical color after I had asked how many Apostles there were. That being said, if the answer I was looking for was "Jesus" or "love," I could always rely on our kindergarteners to come through!

While "Jesus" and "love" were usually not the answers I was looking for, those two responses summarize the faith of a baptized Christian in its essential dimension: relationship. Being a Christian is about falling in love with Jesus, being in a relationship with the living God and freely choosing to love him. Everything else—rituals, sacraments, prayers, devotions, everything—is a means to that end: falling in love with the Lord. The question we are focusing on this week is about this relationship. When we acknowledge our belovedness and our relationship to God as his children, we experience freedom. When we worship anything other than the Creator, we become enslaved, burdened, and weighed down.

When we think about God in terms of a relationship, an interesting twist is put on the dimensions of our faith that some might perceive as legalistic. Think about what you have been taught in terms of the rules and regulations of the faith: the commandments, what counts as prayer or sin, how often one should go to confession, how late can you arrive at Mass, etc. In one sense, these are important things to know and help provide a framework for what it means to be a Christian in a universal Church. However, all of the answers to these questions are rooted in one thing: a response of love. If we're looking to understand what it means to reject sin, we must be clear about what it means to accept God. Rejecting sin does not simply mean avoiding evil and following the rules, it perhaps more appropriately means allowing oneself to fall in love with God.

Think about your best friend or your significant other. Do you constantly walk around in fear, trying to avoid gossiping about them? Are you constantly working to keep yourself from being mean to them? Do you ask how many times you need to apologize to them? Can you imagine having a conversation with them and then trying to figure out if talking with them was worth it? Put in a relational context, these questions sound ridiculous. You don't spend time with loved ones to "get something out of it," but simply because you love being together.

When we love someone, we naturally do the things they like and avoid the things they don't because we care for them. In our spiritual lives, is our main goal the avoidance of sin? Or, rather, is it primarily falling in love with Jesus? When we recognize that love is the foundation for avoiding sin, the centrality of our relationship with Christ allows us to see the rules and regulations of our faith as a framework for loving well. This is what it means "to live in the freedom of God's children" (*Rite of Christian Initiation of Adults* [RCIA], 238). It provides a motivation for our actions that keeps the Lord at the forefront, rather than being held captive by fear of punishment. Rejecting sin is simply permitting ourselves to fall more deeply in love with the God who has called us to new life through our Baptism.

When we sin, we are choosing to turn away from the love of God and his presence in our lives and in our relationships with others. This week's invitation to "reject sin" should not be a burden. Yes, it is challenging, but it takes effort to maintain any relationship. This week we are invited to live more fully in the freedom of our relationship with God. Rejecting sin means choosing God, who is constantly choosing us. When we give our time and attention to this relationship, we cooperate with the graces given to us by God at our Baptism and throughout our lives as we participate in the life of the Church.

 ## Witnesses of Faith

At the beginning of Lent, the catechumens (those who are preparing to be baptized at the Easter Vigil), participate in the Rite of Election. This typically happens on the First Sunday of Lent. To prepare for this rite, they spend several months discerning and listening to God's call inviting them to a deeper relationship with him. In the liturgy for the Rite of Election, the bishop addresses the catechumens, saying:

> Since you have already heard the call of Christ, you must now express your response to that call clearly and in the presence of the whole Church. Therefore, do you wish to enter fully into the life of the Church through the sacraments of baptism, confirmation, and the eucharist? (RCIA, 132)

By affirming this call through their consent and participation in this ritual, they are now called the *elect*. This term signifies their recognition, and the Church's, of God's choice in them to become adopted sons and daughters. They make this public response to continue in their journey toward initiation by writing their names in the Book of the Elect at this liturgy.

God has also called and chosen us. At our Baptism, we took on the name "Christian." This name shows that our identity comes from Christ. Through Christ, we become children of God and belong to him. Psalm 139 reminds us of God's intimate relationship with us; he knows our hearts, our strengths, and even our weaknesses. He knows what we've done and what we're going to do. He knew us before we even existed. We grow into this identity by listening to the Holy Spirit's call. The Spirit guides us to choose the love of God over selfish desires. We are led to participate in the sacraments of the Church. All of these choices help us to deepen our relationship with God.

The identity given to us at our Baptism is an indelible mark from God, a permanent invisible mark that cannot be repeated, erased, lost, or taken away. We are forever his. If God speaks our souls into being and sees us as we truly are, can we erase what God has done? So often we name ourselves by our weaknesses or our brokenness. We say things like, "I am a failure" or "I am not worthy." We believe the lies we tell ourselves, "I am not smart enough" or "I am not beautiful enough" or perhaps even "I am unlovable." Satan calls us by our brokenness and our sin; God call us by our name. Even though we do experience brokenness and temptation, we are God's children *now and always*. It is true that original sin destroyed the original communion human beings had with God. We still see the effects of sin in the world today. However, Christ's Paschal Mystery overcame the break in relationship that happened because of original sin. Christ offers us a way back to God. This journey of salvation was initiated at our Baptism when we were claimed for Christ and named a child of God. It continues as we reaffirm our choice to love God and reject sin, cooperating with the grace that God pours out on us. When we can see ourselves through the eyes of the Father, we find that it is easier to be true to that God-given identity rather than finding an alternative identity in an unfulfilling life of sin.

This week's question reminds us that the prayer, fasting, and charity we choose to do during the Lenten season should be reflected throughout our entire life. When we choose to do these things, we are rejecting sin and accepting the love of God. Our actions help others to see Christ's presence in the world and can inspire them to respond to God's call as well. Even if you do not have any elect in your parish community this Lent, there are thousands of elect around the world who are discerning God's voice in their hearts and attempting to clarify that call so as to truly live their lives in freedom as children of God. As we witness the everyday choices of those around us who are responding to God's love by committing to the Christian life, we are moved by their testimony to reconsider our own choices. Lent is a time to reflect on these things and respond to God's call by entering more deeply into our relationship with him.

 ## Praying through the Week

Use the following questions and Scripture passages to guide your prayer time as you reflect on this week's theme.

1. How does looking at Lent through the lens of Baptism transform or enrich my understanding of this season? How do my daily actions show that I am a child of God?

2. What is the focus of my prayer, God, or myself? If prayer is my response to God's love for me, how might I use this time to fall more deeply in love with God? Is my Lenten plan based on God's plan for me?

3. Do I believe that God loves me unconditionally, independent of what I do or do not do, of my achievements or failures? How does God's image of me as beloved, cherished, and known compete with my self-image? How can I respond to God's endless mercy and love?

Deuteronomy 7:6–9   Sirach 17:24–29
Psalm 32:3–7   Isaiah 1:16–18
Psalm 51:3–10   Matthew 6:1-8
Psalm 139:1–16

WEEK 2

Do you reject the glamour of evil, and refuse to be mastered by sin?

Rite of Christian Initiation of Adults, 238

 ## Baptized in Christ

When people who wish to celebrate the sacrament of Reconciliation face-to-face walk into my confessional, before I begin the sacrament, I typically will just smile and greet them briefly, asking them how they are doing while they are taking their seat. People frequently joke, "Well, I'm *here* again . . . so I can't be doing *that* well, right, Father?" The first couple of times that this happened, I laughed it off. Then I began to notice how often people made comments like this. I started to think more about how we view our conversion, our coming back to God. When we talk about the sacraments, we usually use the verb "celebrate": we celebrate Mass or the Eucharist, we celebrate Baptism, we celebrate Anointing of the Sick, etc. If we always feel miserable for needing the grace of the sacrament of Reconciliation, can we really say that our acts of confession and reconciliation are a *celebration*?

The deciding factor will mostly likely be our image and understanding of God. Perhaps the God we have been formed to envision is a God who is somewhat removed from our daily lives, one whose primary role is to keep a record of our sins. In that case, it's no wonder why someone would not be "celebrating" Reconciliation. It's hard enough to admit our areas of sin to ourselves; who would want to go over his or her score card with the almighty God? On the other hand, if we can recognize a God who is intimately connected with us, whose love sustains our every breath, whose strongest desire is for us to come home to life in his presence— how can we not truly *celebrate* this sacrament?

Reconciliation, then, is a sacrament that celebrates the triumph of God's grace and mercy over our individual sinfulness. We certainly will feel remorse for our sins, and no doubt, there is always a heaviness on our hearts as we make our way into the confessional. At the same time, however, we recognize that it is the grace of the Holy Spirit working in us that inspires our journey back into the arms of the merciful Father. We began this journey in our Baptism, where God's grace cleansed us of our sins. From that moment on, we were filled with a desire to be more completely his. *This* is nothing to be ashamed of. God's plan does not require us to heal ourselves before coming to him. Rather, in the midst of our sinfulness, God invites us to ask for healing and to trust that he will accomplish his plan in us in his time. *This* is cause for celebration!

Beyond the sacrament of Reconciliation, we celebrate our need for God at every Mass. Before we seek the Lord in his Word and in the Eucharist, we celebrate the Penitential Act in which we acknowledge our sin and ask for forgiveness and mercy. Even in this brief prayer, we are being moved from sin to new life by grace. After we call to mind our faults and failings that work against our baptismal identity as children of God, we pray a litany of forgiveness: "Lord, have mercy"; "Christ, have mercy"; "Lord, have mercy" (*The Roman Missal*). What is the focus of this prayer? It is not ourselves and our sinfulness, but our faith in the awesome power and mercy of our Risen Lord. Coupled with this cry of mercy, we hear invocations describing God as healer of wounds and divisions, sustainer of life, and mighty and powerful. Notice, we're not praying, "We are the worst. Lord, have mercy." Or, "We are horrible disciples. Christ, have mercy." No. While we might be tempted occasionally to pray in those ways on our own, all of the prayers in the Mass are proclamations of the power of Christ over sin and death. The focus in the Penitential Act is not simply on our need, but it is on Christ, who is moving our sin to something of life and glory. This prayer is both an acknowledgement of our sin and a profession of faith in the redemptive work of Jesus Christ. This action helps to prepare us to receive the Body and Blood of Christ, which sustains us on our journey back to God.

When we allow ourselves to be open to God's mercy and grace in the sacraments, we find renewed strength to keep our focus on Christ as we enter into deeper communion with him. God is building on the grace of our Baptism in order to free us from being mastered by sin and bring us closer to him. But, we have to cooperate. This season of Lent helps to develop in us a pattern of daily living. We acknowledge that we are neither saved by our own merits nor disqualified by our sinfulness. The work of becoming holy is God's work in us. We are incorporated into Christ's Body by virtue of our Baptism. We can celebrate the sacraments because the Holy Spirit leads us to participate in them. We are drawn closer to God. In all of these things, we are given the strength to overcome the hold sin can have on us.

 ## Witnesses of Faith

The elect are now in their second week of what is called the Period of Purification and Enlightenment. This period traditionally coincides with Lent and begins with the Rite of Election (usually celebrated on the First Sunday of Lent). This is a time of intentional reflection and spiritual preparation. Through prayer, liturgies, and discernment, the elect are strengthened in their resolve to turn away from sin, repent, and allow God's grace to overflow into their lives. This time ends at the Easter Vigil, where the elect will encounter the grace of God in the sacraments of Baptism, Confirmation, and the Eucharist.

In 2 Corinthians 12:5–10, St. Paul shares with us an encounter with a struggle, a "thorn" in his side. We do not know what this thorn is but it is clear that it is weighing Paul down, so much so that he begs the Lord to remove it from his life, not once but three times. We do this same thing as we approach God in our cycles of sin. Surprisingly, in response to St. Paul, God does not remove the thorn. Instead, the Lord says to him, "My grace is sufficient for you, for power is made perfect in weakness" (2 Corinthians 12:9). This passage reminds us that the grace of Baptism is constantly working to sustain us throughout our lives. In the midst of our crosses, God raises us up to hope and newness of life through Christ's victory over sin and death.

This second question of the Renunciation of Sin, which we are considering this week, admits that sin is glamorous and tempting. Lent invites us to journey with the elect as we reexamine our own tendencies to sin. When we overlook our sins and ignore the faults that have become habits, we become more entrapped by them. In our daily prayers, and as we prepare for the sacrament of Reconciliation, it is important to examine all aspects of our lives with honesty so that the Holy Spirit can show us the areas of sin and doubt that we need to take to our merciful Father. When we celebrate the sacrament of Reconciliation, we resolve—as we pray in the Act of Contrition—to amend our lives and begin anew with God's help.

In spite of this, oftentimes we keep coming back to the sacrament and confessing the exact same sins. In these cases, our sins become a thorn that keeps needling us. We can fall into despair and try desperately to fix ourselves. The Gospel, however, is not about rolling up our sleeves and trying harder; it's about responding to and cooperating with grace. Sometimes we become so sensitive to what we think God is "not doing," that we don't even think to stop and consider what he *is* doing. We find ourselves at the point of tears as we acknowledge our exhaustion and our inability to live as Christ calls us to in Baptism. And yet, it is the very grace of our Baptism that is providing a deluge of desire for salvation, holiness, greater compassion, and reconciliation. Our desire to be healed and saved from sin is, in and of itself, the prayer of our heart. Just like the elect, we are moved to be more open to accept God's grace working in our lives.

When we focus on him, Jesus teaches us how he is working in us, not despite our sinfulness, but precisely because of it. His "power is made perfect in weakness" (2 Corinthians 12:9). Our baptismal grace gives us power to turn away from sin. When we refuse to be mastered by sin, we refuse to believe Satan's claim that we can fix ourselves and that God has no interest in our lives. We place God's mercy and grace—rather than lies—at the center of our lives. In doing so, we become a witness to others of God's perpetual desire for a relationship with us. We allow God to work through our actions so that others may come to know him. This time of spiritual preparation for the elect reminds us that we too must open ourselves to God's grace so that we have the strength to turn away from the glamour of evil and the temptations of sin.

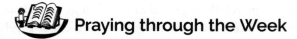 ## Praying through the Week

Use the following questions and Scripture passages to guide your prayer time as you reflect on this week's theme.

1. What is my vision of God? Do I typically pray to God the Father, God the Son, or God the Holy Spirit? How does my understanding of God shape my relationship with him?

2. How do I approach the sacrament of Reconciliation? Do I look forward to it as a celebration of God's mercy and love? Do I dread revealing my failings to God and admitting that I need his help? How can I allow God to work in me instead of my own attempts to fix myself?

3. When have I taken time to notice God's presence in my daily life and in the lives of those around me? How can I pray so that it might be easier to hear God's voice in the midst of my sins? How do my actions reflect my belief that God's grace works within me, not despite my sins but precisely because of them?

Psalm 51:11–19
Psalm 103:1–10
Jeremiah 17:5–8
Joel 2:12–13

John 20:19–23
2 Corinthians 12:5–10
James 4:7–10

WEEK 3

Do you reject Satan, the father of sin and prince of darkness?

Rite of Christian Initiation of Adults, 238

 ## Baptized in Christ

When I was in elementary school, my mom would wake me up every day at 7:00 AM. I would get dressed in my Catholic school uniform and go downstairs to eat breakfast while I watched cartoons. These cartoons would usually feature some scene in which one the characters needed to make a significant decision. A little angel and a little devil would appear out of thin air. Perched on either shoulder of the character, the little angel would try to convince the character to make the morally sound, respectable decision, while the little devil would try to persuade the character to choose to do something bad. "Come on! Do it!" they would both say convincingly. Eventually, the character would grow exhausted from the tension, dust the apparitions from their shoulders, and then decide on a course of action. This can be a helpful visualization in some ways when discerning the real choices we have to make between good and evil. However, this version of cartoon spirituality can lead us to think that there are two contenders of equal strength and power in the ongoing battle for souls. The truth is, God and Satan are not equals.

Satan is not a cartoon character and there is no scenario in which our choosing the path of sin will lead us to a happy ending. Originally created an angel by God, his name was Lucifer, or light-bearer. But as God began to create human beings and revealed his plan for these children to be made in his image and likeness and share in his eternal life, Satan became envious. As a result, he chose to turn away from God and successfully convinced the man and the woman that their Father was not a

God of love but a God of deception. Believing in his lies, human beings became ensnared and enslaved to sin and death. Still today, we are drawn into both through the lies of the prince of darkness.

Then, in the fullness of time, God sent his Word, his Son, into the world. This Word God spoke in silence, in disguise. The Son, who shares in the divinity of God as one person of the Trinity, humbled himself and came to earth as a human being, like us in all things but sin. He is both fully human and fully divine. Out of God's great love for all of creation, Jesus came to redeem us by his death. As Jesus is mocked and betrayed, suffers and dies, Satan thinks himself victorious. However, three days later, Christ is raised from the tomb in glorious majesty, destroying death forever and opening the gates of heaven to the children of God once more.

Because of the work of redemption accomplished on the cross by Jesus, no suffering is in vain; death is never an end. There is no cross that we will ever encounter in this world that cannot have meaning or purpose, or cannot be used by God for our sanctification and for the salvation of the world. Our Baptism places us within the shelter of Christ's cross. Because of what Jesus has accomplished on the cross, we come to recognize God's power not only in obvious works of glory and splendor, but most especially in realms of sin and despair. The cross is the symbol of victory and life, not just for Christ but for us as well.

Cartoon spirituality communicates that the contenders for our souls are equal in power. It fails to acknowledge that we are created good; even before our Baptism, we are all created in the image and likeness of God! Baptism and the grace of the sacraments fortify our ability to choose the good. Satan is a created being who has been *completely* defeated by the blood of the Lamb, our God-made-flesh. Death has lost. Sin has been conquered. Darkness is banished. And while Satan can certainly tempt us, he has no power. In order for us to fight against temptation and sin, almighty God supplies us with grace through the gift of his very life. We receive this grace in our Baptism, where we are claimed for Christ and made sons and daughters of God. We are made his holy people, anointed priest, prophet, and king to proclaim God's power and reject Satan. This is the task of all the baptized, to live abundantly in the light of God's grace, for Jesus has already saved us from our sins.

Witnesses of Faith

As the elect continue in the Period of Purification and Enlightenment, they celebrate the First Scrutiny on this Sunday. The Scrutinies are celebrated on the Third, Fourth, and Fifth Sundays of Lent as rites of healing and strengthening for the elect. The elect are invited into deeper self-reflection in order to more clearly reveal areas of weakness and sin. With the aid of the prayers of the assembly in the form of intercessions and prayers of minor exorcism said by the priest or deacon, the Church calls upon God to fortify the elect in the Spirit so that they may turn away from sin.

In these prayers of exorcism, the celebrant asks that these elect might trust in the Lord as the one who saves them from their sins and weaknesses. The elect thirst for the healing and life-giving waters of Baptism, just as the Samaritan woman thirsted for the water of eternal life that Jesus offered (John 4:5–42). The prayers of exorcism then go on to prefigure the themes of the questions we have been reflecting on as part of the Renunciation of Sin before Baptism. The Church prays that the elect may be set free "from the spirit of deceit," "from the slavery of sin," and from "Satan's crushing yoke [in] exchange [for] the gentle yoke of Jesus" (RCIA, 154). It is made clear to the elect and to the assembly during these important rites that what saves us is not our perfection, but our willingness to be healed by Jesus' Paschal Mystery.

As baptized members of God's family, we open ourselves to Jesus' healing by reconciling ourselves with God. When we come to be reconciled with God, particularly in the sacrament of Reconciliation, we do not need to worry about "if" God will forgive us. Jesus has already died for our sins. Our primary focus, by way of an examination of our lives and our consciences, is to offer to the Lord honestly and directly those places in our hearts that have turned away from his love and are weighed down by the emptiness that comes from being inauthentic to our baptismal call.

Being aware of the Good News of Jesus' Paschal Mystery and immersing ourselves in his love makes our conversion possible because it gives us reason to hope, reason to surrender. It gives us the sure knowledge that we do not respond the call to holiness without the help of grace. The First Scrutiny of the elect reminds us that we can always call upon the Holy

Spirit to guide us in our daily actions. When we cooperate with this work of salvation within us, we proclaim our choice of God over Satan. All of the seemingly small choices we make each day are being formed together into one testimony of the eternity we hope to experience, eternal life with God. God gives us everything we need in order to choose him in freedom and reject sin. Every experience in our lives can lead us closer to God. We cannot be afraid of living a life of holiness and integrity. By the witness of our own choices, others come to see how God's Spirit is still present in the world. We don't need a cartoon angel to show us the way; we have the witness of Christ, of our brothers and sisters in faith, the saints, and all of creation to help us see the path to God.

This week, as we walk with the elect through this First Scrutiny and as we recommit to rejecting sin, we are invited to confess not just our errors but to profess profound faith in the God who desires to bring us home to himself. At some point during this week, the elect will participate in a liturgy in which they receive the Creed. Upon hearing our beliefs voiced by the assembly, the elect will be invited to memorize these words of faith and recite them publicly as truth on the day of their Baptism. This text and living faith is yet another entry point for deeper enlightenment and reflection.

Every time we profess our faith at Mass, we recall the incredible love story that God has written and continues to author with our cooperation. We know the ending of this story but we do not simply arrive in heavenly perfection overnight. Just as the process of initiation for these elect is sequential, we too take steps toward deeper communion each and every day as we trust in the promise of the Risen Savior. God's grace builds on our nature and unfolds gradually throughout our life.

Praying through the Week

Use the following questions and Scripture passages to guide your prayer time as you reflect on this week's theme.

1. Celebrate the sacrament of Reconciliation during this season of Lent. What is the grace my heart most desires at this time in order to fight against temptation and sin? If Reconciliation is not a regular part of my prayer life, how does its connection to my baptismal identity encourage me to celebrate this sacrament more often?

2. What am I most afraid to talk about with God? How can I bring more integrity into my relationship with God by acknowledging and reflecting on these areas of woundedness or shame? How can I cleanse these dark areas with the life-giving water of my Baptism?

3. This week, pray an examination of conscience each day, preferably before going to bed. As I replay my day from beginning to end, what were the ways that I chose God by my thoughts, words, and actions? In what ways did I reject God? End with a prayer of thanksgiving for the day's blessings and for God's presence.

Genesis 1:1–3 and
John 1:1–5
Genesis 1:26–31
Psalm 143

John 4:5–42
Romans 5:6–8
Romans 10:8–13
1 Peter 3:18

Part II: **Turn toward God**

In **Part I: Turn Away from Sin,** we considered the questions that make up the Renunciation of Sin before the rite of Baptism. Over the past three weeks, we have walked with the elect and, with them, have considered the invitation to turn away from sin in light of the grace of Baptism.

During the First Week of Lent, we reflected on the way our lives of faith are responses to a living relationship with the God who first loved us into being. Through Baptism, we have been made sons and daughters of God. Nothing that we ever do can make him love us more completely; nothing that we ever do can disqualify us from his love and forgiveness.

When we choose to reject sin, we allow ourselves to live in the freedom of God's love.

During the Second Week of Lent, we considered the fountain of mercy and grace contained within the celebration of the sacrament of Reconciliation, which helps us to reconnect with our baptismal grace. Through the process of reconciling ourselves to God, we come to see the Holy Spirit's work more clearly in our lives and go beyond the failures of our own efforts. Every time we recognize God's work present in the world around us, we reject the temptations placed before us and refuse to be mastered by sin. Our confession of sins becomes a profession of faith, that our God remains forever faithful.

Finally, during the Third Week of Lent, we reflected on the power of God over sin and death. Through Christ's Paschal Mystery, our suffering is overcome and finds purpose to be used for the glory of God. By proclaiming the Good News of Jesus' saving actions and the power of God's grace we received in Baptism, we reject Satan and all his lies.

These themes of our relationship with God, his actions, and his faithfulness help us to turn away from sin on our Lenten journey. Our rejection of sin in light of God's love and faithfulness forms us in a pattern for daily living. We strive to be people of hope who trust that every cross comes with resurrection. Likewise, the elect have continued their journey toward the reception of the sacraments of initiation. They have participated in the Rite of Election and are now in the Period of Purification and Enlightenment. Their witness and presence in our communities inspire those of us who have already been baptized to return our hearts to God and deepen our relationship with him.

In this second half of Lent, we will consider how we turn toward God. We will move deeply into the work of conversion and permit God to change us more profoundly by his presence. We will consider our Lenten journey through the lens of the three questions of the Profession of Faith, which occurs after the Renunciation of Sin when we renew our baptismal promises. These questions are drawn from the Apostles' Creed, in which we profess our belief in the Triune God (Father, Son, and Holy Spirit) and in the Church established by Jesus Christ. These questions help us to connect our baptismal identity with our lifelong vocation to eternal life with God. As we consider our immersion into the life of God and the community of faith through the font of Baptism, we also pray for the elect as they become more aware of their deep need for God's grace and mercy. Spending time in prayer and reflection during these final weeks of Lent will help us to renew our baptismal vows at Easter and profess our faith in God the Father, God the Son, and God the Holy Spirit.

WEEK 4

Do you believe in God, the Father almighty, creator of heaven and earth?

Rite of Christian Initiation of Adults, 239

 ### Baptized in Christ

As a priest, I think infant Baptism might be the easiest sacrament to celebrate; everyone is so joyful! Rarely are parents worried or nervous about how the liturgy will turn out or where people will sit or their meal plans afterwards. Their child might cry or fuss or sleep but whatever happens, happens. Their attention isn't on the other guests or anything else; they are focused on their son or daughter, whom they have brought to be welcomed into God's Church by water and the Holy Spirit.

I frequently catch myself being captivated by the emotion and the bright, smiling eyes of the hope-filled parents and godparents. I can't help but be moved as I watch them entrust their most precious gift to the Lord and to the community of faith. I find myself calling to mind the great surrender and trust of Hannah as she gave her long-awaited, firstborn son to God in the temple (1 Samuel 1:1—2:11). I often joke that had I been called to a different vocation, I would have been a terrible father in the sense that I would never let my kids grow up or leave the house. Ever. No dating, no parties, no moving out . . . just stay where I can protect you and love you and keep you safe, and everything will be fine. Right?

We don't want to see our kids get hurt. We will stop at nothing to make sure their hearts never get broken. And yet, even though we feel like never letting go so as to protect them from any harm that might come their way, we know that simply is not how life works. We have to let go for their sake and for ours. For children to mature in wisdom and grace, they have to be entrusted to their heavenly Father. As much love as we have for our children, our nieces, our nephews, or any child entrusted to our care, God's love for them (and us) far surpasses any human capacity for love. We know that their faith will only develop through their own encounters with Christ. They will need the strength and community found in God's love to continue in the midst of their brokenness and in the crosses of life. They will need to learn how to be people of hope. Baptism is a sacrament of trust; believing in the promise of the Father to care for his children. We entrust ourselves and our children to God so that he may bring his work to fulfillment in us, while keeping us safe from the poison of sin.

The first question in the Profession of Faith, which we are considering this week, centers on the first person of the Blessed Trinity. Two images are presented about God in this creedal statement. He is our Father and the Creator of all that is. At Jesus' own baptism we hear the voice of God, whose Spirit, as at the beginning of creation, hovered over the water as the Father says of Christ: "This is my beloved Son, with whom I am well pleased" (Matthew 3:17). The Trinity acts as one and is present at our own Baptism, as we are baptized in the name of the Father, the Son, and the Holy Spirit.

Christ did not need to be baptized so that he would be cleansed of sins; he was without sin, perfect in holiness. Rather, his baptism purified the waters of Baptism for us, so that we too could become God's sons and daughters, adopted in the Spirit. The font of Baptism, then, is the womb of the Church. All those called by God to enter the waters of rebirth are transformed into a new creation and they are born again of water and the Holy Spirit. These waters, made holy by Christ, make us holy, temples of God's divine Spirit. God's work of sanctification begins to take effect in our lives.

God the Father sends his Son, the Word, into creation (see John 1:1–5, 14). That Word holds within itself the potential to be implanted, to be taken in, to be cultivated and nourished, and to come to birth. The Word, Jesus Christ, is the Good News that fertilizes the Church and gives us new life. By our baptismal identity as adopted sons and daughters of God, we are called to share the Word with others. In doing so, we cooperate with the Holy Spirit and lead others to Christ so that they may become one with him in the Spirit. We are made a chosen race, a royal priesthood, a people belonging to the Father.

In our new birth in Baptism, we receive an indelible mark of grace that cannot be lost or repeated; it marks us as God's own. Our sins are forgiven by God's abundant grace and love. As we are incorporated into the Body of Christ, God makes us into the Church, renewing this building made of living stones that has Christ as the cornerstone. In Baptism, we are invited to surrender our life of sin to put on Christ and bear the name of Christian. In our unity and communion with God, we are being transformed to resemble more closely the image and likeness of the Creator.

Witnesses of Faith

Our worship is noticeably different this weekend as we celebrate Laetare Sunday, the Fourth Sunday in Lent. The Latin word *laetare*, which comes from the Entrance Antiphon in *The Roman Missal* for this Sunday, means "rejoice." We celebrate our liturgy with muted fanfare, perhaps with different music and the use of rose-colored vestments instead of violet. These shifts in environment and worship at this halfway point in Lent provide a brief intermission from our regular seasonal rituals as we experience a foretaste of the rejoicing that will accompany the upcoming Easter celebrations. Together with the elect, we are encouraged, liturgically speaking, to continue in our resolve to turn away from sin. In the midst of our disciplines of prayer, fasting, and almsgiving, we recognize that the day of our rebirth draws near.

This Sunday, the elect participate in the Second Scrutiny. The Gospel reading for this liturgy is the story of Jesus' healing of the man born blind (John 9:1–41). Once again, the assembly intercedes for the elect, this time asking that God's light of truth shine throughout the world. The prayers of minor exorcism invoke Jesus as the "unfailing light," who "cast[s] out the darkness of hatred and lies" from our sight (RCIA, 168). Along with the elect, we pray to be liberated from hatred, personal and social sin, and the masks we put on that blind us to the love of God. Together we pray for deliverance from unbelief, that we might behold God.

Far beyond the sight of this present age, we ask to behold the vision of God's Kingdom, where his justice and mercy will reign. When we see as God sees, we are able to recognize more clearly our own dignity and that of all people. Through the gifts of the Holy Spirit, wisdom, understanding, counsel, fortitude, knowledge, piety, and holy fear, we are better prepared to envision the Kingdom of God. When we see with the eyes of hope and grace, we can work to transform the world by our witness to be more like the vision of God's heavenly Kingdom.

We constantly pray for the strength to live in this way as children of God. It is not always easy to remain faithful to the vision of God in the face of the things that blind us to God's love. Mary is a beautiful Lenten model for us as we pray to see all of our crosses with the eyes of hope. Mary is called upon many times in her life to look at that which might cause in us spiritual blindness: pain, fear, uncertainty, death, destruction, silence. Rather than running away, Mary runs to the cross and embraces it quite literally as she stands with the most precious gift she has: her only son. She offers him to the Father as she chooses to look beyond what is right in front of her eyes, to see with the eyes of God. In all moments, Mary believes and trusts in God's faithfulness and opens herself to the grace of what God is unfolding.

We cannot run from the cross. Like Mary, we are inevitably called to take it up and follow Christ. His cross and his suffering, however, do not end in death. When we take up our crosses, we also take up the hope of new life. These cannot be separated. The crosses we bear will surface many times throughout the course of our life. Nevertheless, as we acknowledge the spiritual blindness that clouds our vision, the grace of our adoption in Christ instills in us the virtue of hope that we have in knowing ourselves as children of the Father.

 ## Praying through the Week

Use the following questions and Scripture passages to guide your prayer time as you reflect on this week's theme.

1. Do I entrust myself to God the Father? In what ways do I entrust others to beloved God? What are the things that stand in the way of this trust? How do my prayers and actions reflect my trust in God?

2. Do I believe that I have been made a new creation in Baptism and am a beloved child of God? When am I most aware of the reality that my body houses God's Spirit? In what ways does recalling this identity call me to

conversion? How does it call me to share the vision of God's Kingdom with others?

3. What cross or crosses am I carrying? How does the grace of my Baptism lead me to a deeper understanding of what God is accomplishing within me? How can Mary be an intercessor and prayer partner for me as I learn to see my crosses as an opportunity for a more profound relationship with God?

1 Samuel 1:20–28   John 9
Psalm 33:6–15   Galatians 3:26–27
Luke 2:25–35   Titus 3:4–7
John 3:20–21

WEEK 5

Do you believe in Jesus Christ, his only Son, our Lord who was born of the Virgin Mary, was crucified, died and was buried, rose from the dead, and is now seated at the right hand of the Father?

Rite of Christian Initiation of Adults, 239

 ## Baptized in Christ

A few years ago, I was ministering at one of our Holy Cross schools in Canto Grande, Peru. Fe y Alegría Nº 25, in the district of San Juan de Lurigancho, educates some 4,000 primary and secondary students. My role was to assist with some of the high school sections of English, theology, and social studies. One day, my class was comparing and contrasting views of the afterlife, and the variety of customs and traditions that stem from those beliefs.

In Canto Grande, as is the case in many regions of Latin America, burial takes place very quickly after death occurs. Typically, only a day or two passes before the body of the deceased is interred. The wake or the vigil before the burial takes place in the family home, and no embalming techniques are employed. I shared with my students that, in the United

States, a funeral usually takes place a few days, if not a week or so, after someone dies. We typically try to gather together our family members who live throughout the state or the country so that all can be together when the life of the deceased is celebrated. Another factor in the delayed burial would be the amount of days it takes to cremate or embalm the body. I explained that if embalming was chosen, it is done in such a way that we try to make the deceased look as though they were merely sleeping, wearing their favorite outfit with their hair styled, etc. I was surprised to learn that my students found this quite odd: "You do *what*? That's so weird! Why are you acting as though they were still alive? They're clearly dead!"

Their reaction, coming from a cultural context that was not my own, opened my eyes to the fact that some of us really don't like death. Our culture goes to extreme lengths to avoid even the idea of death; there are many anti-aging products on the market, the language we use to talk about death glosses over its reality, and our deceased don't even look deceased. All of these customs and practices point to the notion that we, as a society, struggle to come to terms with our own mortality. And yet, when death is looked at through the eyes of faith, it is not the end, it is a new beginning. It is really a new birth, a passageway to eternal life. Still, death is never easy when it comes to the loss, sadness, and adjustments experienced by us who remain. In these moments of grief and sorrow, it becomes painfully evident that we are not meant for this world.

The second question presented in our prebaptismal Profession of Faith describes Jesus and the centrality of the Paschal Mystery. If the whole basis for Baptism is Jesus Christ, then his death is central to our reflection on this sacrament. Jesus' death is the result of his complete obedience, trust, love, and radical, self-emptying humility before God the Father (see Philippians 2:5–11). Out of love for us and for all of creation, he utters the words, "Father, if you are willing, take this cup away from me; still, not my will but yours be done" (Luke 22:42). In the midst of his tears and agony, he takes upon himself the burden of the entire world and our sin, and he allows himself to be murdered.

This incredible hope and trust in the Father's will brings about the work of redemption for us. Through the blood and water flowing from his pierced side, Christ blessed the Church so that we might be born anew in the waters of Baptism and inherit eternal life. We celebrate Christ's sacrifice in all of our sacraments and at the Mass, every time we gather in prayer, and every time we call ourselves Christian. Still, the heaviness and sting of death remains. As Christians, we share in the Easter joy of the disciples—we know that Christ has conquered sin and death so we struggle to accept the reality of death in our lives and the world around us. But we can take comfort in knowing that in the silence of the tomb, death is changed forever. The glory of the Resurrection and Ascension overcomes the darkness of sin and death that keeps us from fully living as sons and daughters of God. We live in the light. Through our Baptism, we die to sin and rise to new life in Christ.

Witnesses of Faith

In this last week of Lent before Holy Week, the elect participate in the Third Scrutiny after reflecting on the story of Jesus' raising of Lazarus from the dead (John 11:1–45). The miracle of Lazarus coming back to life gives us some small sense of what is to come in Jesus' own death. Whereas Lazarus was revived but would die again, Jesus' death is part of the Resurrection and God's plan for the salvation of the world. The prayers of minor exorcism over the elect speak of these themes. In them, the Church asks the Lord "to snatch us from the realm of death" and bring us to an abundant life and final resurrection by the grace of the sacraments (RCIA, 175). We pray for deliverance "from the spirit of corruption" and "the slavery of Satan," whose mission it is to contaminate the goodness of the world made by God (RCIA, 175).

Later this week, the elect will continue to reflect on eternal life in the Kingdom of God by being presented with the Lord's Prayer. Together with the assembly, they will hear the words of the prayer that Jesus taught us, calling on God our Father (Matthew 6:9–13). Like the Creed presented during the Third Week of Lent, this prayer will become a foundation for the elect to continue building their relationship with the Lord and the Church. In this prayer, we pray to be a people who possess unwavering trust in God's will, even in the face of death and temptation.

Areas of death and loss are fertile ground for God to display his power of healing and the gift of new life. We see this taking place in the lives of the elect and all those who open themselves to God's presence. We are reminded that small deaths are part of our daily lives: interacting kindly with people who annoy us and push our buttons, complementing a person rather than gossiping about them, allowing someone to go in front of us who does not deserve to be first, making the choice to pray even when we do not feel like it. We face these and other small deaths when we overcome our selfish desires or the tendency to rely on self rather than God. Uniting all of our sufferings and areas of loss with those of Christ affords us the grace to be strengthened by the One who has conquered death. Christ teaches us to call out to our Father, who will bring us to new life in every situation.

As baptized sons and daughters of God, we call upon the Father every time we celebrate the Eucharist. The Lord's Prayer challenges us to accept one of the most difficult spiritual "deaths" that will confront us in this life: the forgiveness of those who trespass against us. Mindful that there can be no resurrection without the cross, we are invited to confront the hurt we have received or even inflicted upon others. Whether it be our worst enemies, our friends, our family members, God, or even ourselves, the work of forgiveness is patterned on the death and Resurrection of Christ. Forgiveness is a choice, a decision. It is a process and takes place in stages. We must let anger and resentment die so we can cooperate more fully with God's grace along each small step as we move toward complete healing and reconciliation. When we act with forgiveness, we become witnesses of the grace of Baptism that moves us to place our complete trust in God's power, mercy, and love.

Just as the Son of God died and was buried, at our Baptism, we were plunged into the depths of the water, into the emptiness and loneliness of the tomb, and died with Christ. Every time we bless ourselves with holy water or renew our baptismal promises, we are reminded that we must daily die to ourselves so that we can live for Christ and share in the eternal life of God. We die to our former ways of life, our sin, and a life without companionship and communion. We die to everlasting death. When we participate in the sacraments and open ourselves to the Holy Spirit working in our lives, we rise with Christ from the darkness of the tomb. As we journey with the elect this week, we examine our lives in the light of the Paschal Mystery and call upon God our Father to lead us all to his Kingdom.

 **Praying through the Week**

Use the following questions and Scripture passages to guide your prayer time as you reflect on this week's theme.

1. As I come to accept death in its many dimensions, what am I being asked to surrender so that God can possess my entire being? How does Christ's life enter into areas of my life that are in the darkness of sin and death? How can I ask God to strengthen my desire to forgive others so that I am no longer trapped by anger or resentment?

2. In the rich history of our Christian tradition, Baptism is understood as both a womb and a tomb. (You might want to reread Week 4 as you consider the following questions.) Which image most resonates with me at this time? What might this reveal about the ways God is inviting me to cooperate with his grace?

3. The Lord's Prayer is a model of prayer for the elect and for us as disciples of Jesus. On a sheet of paper, make two columns. In the first column, write out the words of the Our Father. In the second column, rewrite each sentence of the prayer in your own words. Throughout the week, take time to reflect on each line of the prayer. How do these words that I pray so often have new meaning in my day-to-day life?

Psalm 130
Matthew 6:9–13
John 11:1–45
Romans 6:1–11

Ephesians 5:8–14
Philippians 2:5–11
Colossians 2:9–15

Do you believe in the Holy Spirit, the holy catholic Church, the communion of saints, the forgiveness of sins, the resurrection of the body, and life everlasting?

Rite of Christian Initiation of Adults, 239

 ## Baptized in Christ

My experience in preparing engaged couples to celebrate the sacrament of Marriage has uncovered a number of shifts in the ways that people are choosing to plan their wedding liturgies. First, rather than not seeing each other before Mass, some couples have chosen to simply walk down the aisle together as the ministers of the sacrament while a gathering hymn is sung (just like a regular Mass). Before the Mass begins, they stand in the entry of the church, greeting their guests as they enter. Second, with regard to seating, more and more couples are not having their families sit on one side of the church or the other. Since their sacrament will celebrate their unity in God, family and friends from the "groom's side" and the "bride's side" are encouraged to sit together (just as at a regular Mass). The congregation, then, also reflects the unity and communion of the love of God that is being mirrored by this couple.

When I've asked couples about their motivation for these plans, which tend to go against the cultural norms we see so often in movies or in other ceremonies, they have generally responded by saying something about being part of a community, part of a whole. They see their vocation as a celebration not belonging to them but to the Church. They hope to show a joyful witness of Christ's love, which always unites us to Christ and one communion of faith. They desire that their ceremony show forth that same witness. I'm always moved by these sorts of responses because they are directly rooted in the grace of our Baptism, in what it means to live a Christian life in communion with God and others.

When we are baptized, we become children of God. We enter into communion with the Father, the Son, and the Holy Spirit and, through them, we are joined to the community of the faithful. The sacrament of Baptism involves the whole community of faith, not just the individuals who are recipients of the sacraments. While the person being baptized is clearly affected by the grace they receive, we are all impacted. The newly baptized Christian is incorporated into the entire community of believers, not just at our parish or in the Roman Catholic Church, but all who make up the Body of Christ—the Church—throughout the world and in heaven. We are called Catholics because our faith is shared with a "catholic," meaning universal, family of believers. The Body of Christ includes *all* who have been baptized in the name of the Father, Son, and Holy Spirit. The communion of saints, who already stand in the eternal presence of God, received in their Baptism the gift of eternal life and a place as members of the Body of Christ. We are brought together into the one Body through the Holy Spirit, who animates our life and our communion. Our local community, believers throughout the world, and the communion of saints grow more alive and more diverse every day as people are baptized into this family of faith. As baptized members, we consider it our privilege to welcome these children of God.

When we renew our baptismal promises, renouncing sin and professing our faith in God, we affirm our role in the Body of Christ and acknowledge the Holy Spirit's presence in our lives. In Baptism and in our ongoing participation in the sacraments, we have the grace of forgiveness of our sins. We live in hope of eternal life with God and the resurrection of our bodies when Christ comes again. This is what God promises to us. He will transform us from within and give us the grace we need to live as his holy people. We experience in a profound way communion with God and others through God's unending covenant of love as he claims us for himself.

 ## Witnesses of Faith

This week, the elect begin their final preparations for the sacraments of initiation. On Holy Saturday, they will spend their day fasting and prayerfully reflecting on the upcoming Easter Vigil. They participate in the Preparation Rites, where the catechists and those who supported them in their journey to Christ come together in prayer. Here they will reflect on the community they are about to become a part of. They will listen to God's Word as it is broken open. Then they will have an opportunity to recite the Creed that they had been presented with during the Third Week of Lent. Additional rites can be celebrated, all of which include prayers for God's continued work of grace in the elect, as they approach the sacraments of Baptism, Confirmation, and the Eucharist.

We too are encouraged to spend time fasting and in prayerful reflection this week as we consider our renewal of baptismal promises. We recognize that our participation in the sacraments is a witness to others of the intimate union between Christ, the Church, and the family of believers. Jesus does not begin his ministry of calling others to himself and building up the Kingdom of God until after his baptism. Here again, we see Baptism leading to the formation of a community centered on God's Word and animated by the power of the Holy Spirit. The waters of our own Baptism call to us to recognize our unity in Christ and with one another.

We become the Church, a living body of believers. All of the sacraments have a communal aspect. It is easy to see sacraments such as Baptism, Confirmation, Eucharist, Marriage, and Holy Orders as communal celebrations, taking place in the house of God. Likewise, when one member hurts, we are all affected. In cases of illness, we bring this person into our personal and public prayer, we visit them with the Eucharist from our communal liturgies, and we celebrate the sacrament of Anointing of the Sick with them. In cases of sin, the communion amongst ourselves and God and ourselves and the community of faith is injured. Before we can stand with integrity before the Eucharist and be in communion with Christ and his Church, we confess our sins to God and ask for his forgiveness through the ministry of the priest in the sacrament of Reconciliation. The priest, standing in the person of Jesus and as a representative of the Church, receives our apology, absolves us through the grace of God, and forgives us on behalf of the Church. Is this not the second half of any apology, to hear that we are forgiven?

We celebrate our incorporation into the Body of Christ at each and every liturgy. We acknowledge this communion and pray for the strength to continue welcoming others into it through our witness. In the Liturgy of the Word, we hear the story of salvation proclaimed and the way it transforms us. In the Liturgy of the Eucharist, we are called to be moved by the presence of Christ in such a way that reflects our union with him and with one another. We are sent out to share what we have received. The presence of the elect energizes us to continue living an authentic witness of our baptismal identity. Each and every Mass is a prayer to live out and to make real the communion of our Baptism, and to engage in mission and ministry as the hands, the feet, and the voice of Christ in this world. Just as the elect act as a witness to God's love drawing people to himself, we stand as witnesses to God's love that is sent out to transform the world into a communion of faith and hope bound together by the Spirit.

As we prepare to renew our own baptismal promises at the end of this most holy of weeks, we enter more deeply into prayer through the liturgies of Christ's life, death, and Resurrection. We find time for silence. We join with other members of the Body of Christ to celebrate the Sacred Paschal Triduum, honoring Christ's Paschal Mystery as the path of our salvation. We pray with and for the elect as they walk the way of the Lord's passion so that they may be prepared to receive God's grace in Baptism, Confirmation, and the Eucharist. The Paschal Mystery is not just the mystery of Jesus; it is the mystery of our new life, death, and resurrection as well. All that Christ accomplishes, he accomplishes in us and throughout the world, now and for ever.

 ## Praying through the Week

Use the following questions and Scripture passages to guide your prayer time as you reflect on this week's theme.

1. What is the link between my Baptism and the call to service in the Church? How is God drawing me to acts of charity and ministry in the Church at this time in my life? How do I contribute to building up the Body of Christ?

2. What part of the Mass most clearly speaks to me of my connection to the Body of Christ? To the communion of saints? In which part of Mass do I experience the deepest connection to my Baptism? How does this lead me to share the Good News with others?

3. Attend the liturgies on Palm Sunday and the Sacred Triduum: Holy Thursday, Good Friday, and the Easter Vigil, at which the elect will be baptized. After each liturgy, consider the question: How did this liturgy affect my understanding and appreciation of my Baptism? What stood out to me about this particular liturgy and how does it connect to my call to live as a child of God?

Monday–Wednesday
Acts 2:38, 42–47
1 Corinthians 12:12–15, 27–30
James 5:16, 19–20

Holy Thursday
Psalm 24:3–6
John 13:1–15
1 Corinthians 13:1–3, 13

Good Friday
Psalm 22
Psalm 31

Holy Saturday
Psalm 16
Psalm 30

Easter Sunday
Acts 10:34–43
1 Peter 2:1–10
1 John 1:1–4

Part III: **Living Your Baptismal Life**

Christ is risen! Alleluia! Having celebrated the triumph of the Paschal Mystery at Easter once more, we, like the first disciples, experience our reason for hope. Our lives are forever changed. Although we have celebrated Easter in years past, each time is a rebirth for us at that moment in time. This Lent we have taken a deeper look at our lives through the lens of the grace that God extends to us in our Baptism. We have considered the times we failed to cooperate with that grace and recognized the times that we allowed it to work through us. We have worked to turn away from sin and toward God, so that we are better able to affirm our faith at Easter.

The elect have also walked in the way of the cross with Jesus as they died to sin, were buried with the Lord in the font of Baptism at the Easter Vigil, and rose with him to Easter joy and unending life. Now called *neophytes*, these newly initiated begin the Period of Mystagogy. During this time, they reflect on what they just celebrated at the Easter Vigil and the significance of their encounter with and participation in the Paschal Mystery. We are invited to do the same, as a community of faith that journeys together toward the Kingdom of God. Our faith, after all, is rooted in more than just the event of the life, death, and Resurrection of Christ. It is rooted in our encounter with it and the way it transforms us. Mystagogy provides space for the newly baptized to unpack the mysteries of salvation alongside the community of believers to which they now belong. It also provides time to consider what their response to this love will be in the context of their local community.

In a way, this idea of mystagogy is how we all should approach our faith. Even though our Baptism may have happened years ago, we are still called to reflect on the working of the Holy Spirit in our lives. We encounter the living Word of God every day. The liturgical year (Advent, Christmas Time, Lent, Easter Time, and Ordinary Time) and every liturgy reminds us that Christ took on flesh, suffered, died, was buried, and rose to new life. Our encounter with his presence encourages us to a life of beatitude, of living the Gospel, and new ways of thinking about our sin and our salvation. We see this happen repeatedly throughout Sacred Scripture when people meet Jesus face-to-face. Christ is our path to salvation; his death is our death, his life our life. Our Lenten journey, forty days in which we considered how God was working to transform us, culminates in a renewed life of faith and discipleship.

The fifty days of Easter Time is a time of mystagogy for us, as we anticipate how the Risen Lord is inviting permanent change, transformation, and healing in our lives. He is calling us to walk boldly out of the tomb and never be the same. Our Lenten call to turn away from sin and to turn toward God continues to call to us throughout the liturgical year. The movement from Lent to Easter is a model for our own life. It invites us to move ever deeper into the mystery of the cross and the hope it brings.

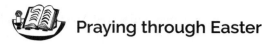 **Praying through Easter**

Throughout this Easter season we are invited to encounter the Risen Lord in the Scriptures, as we hear, week after week, of Christ meeting the disciples where they are, teaching them, and encouraging them to share his Good News with the world. As you journey through Easter, place yourselves in these Gospel stories and consider the following:

- How would you react to Jesus' appearance and actions?

- How would you describe these events to others?

- How is the Risen Lord present in your life today?

- What does this story tell you about your identity as a child of God, who has been baptized into Christ's Paschal Mystery and lives in communion with believers across the world and throughout time?

- How can your words and actions be a witness of the Good News of Christ's triumph over sin and death? What opportunities do you have to journey with others as you turn toward God?

The following reflections are some examples of how you can break open the readings during Easter Time. The Word of God is alive and present in our lives. It invites us to engage it, ask questions, find the answers to what we search for, and meet the Risen Lord.

The Empty Tomb (*Mark 16:1–7*)

Imagine what it was like to be an apostle. Having given your life completely to Jesus, you left your hometown, your job, your family, and all of your friends. More importantly, you trusted him. There is something captivating about his mission and his love and his teaching. You believe it with all of your heart, and you desire that all the world hear and experience this incredible man, the Son of God. But one night your life is forever changed. In the blink of an eye, it seems, Jesus is sharing his last meal with you, he is arrested, he is led through the streets as a criminal, and he is crucified. Within a few hours, the one you gave everything for is dead. There must have been some misunderstanding. How could it end like this? You are heartbroken, disappointed, and scared. You feel lost and without purpose.

And yet, in spite of these feelings, the women go to the tomb to anoint Jesus' body. In spite of the doubts and fears that must have surely been present, they go. They go, even though they don't know how they will reach him, since there was a large stone covering the entrance to the tomb.

Throughout his life, Jesus performed incredible works. At his hands, the hungry were fed, the sick were healed, storms ceased, and the dead were raised. In him, we see that truly nothing is impossible for God. Even from the grave, we see Christ working to lead his followers closer to God. He is resurrected. The stone that hides this truth is rolled away. He allows the disciples to enter into his death so that they can enter into his risen life. Upon entering the tomb, the women are surprised to encounter not death, decay, or a failed mission, but a promise fulfilled, the possibility of hope, the joy of truth, and the victory of the cross.

The crosses in our lives are inevitable, along with the tomb they bring. But God invites us to step into the places of darkness where we expect to find only death and destruction. He takes these tombs we have built by our sins and the lies we choose to believe and uses them to surprise us by the hope of the cross. The stone is rolled away so that we might go in, and upon entering the silence of the tomb, find the truth of the presence of the Risen Lord. We share this joy with others, so that in their own "tombs" they too might find Christ.

Doubting Thomas (*John 20:19–31*)

Every year, on the Second Sunday of Easter, we hear the story of "Doubting Thomas." Even though we are asked to believe in Christ's Resurrection without seeing the Risen Lord in person, just as Thomas was, we have the advantage of having access to Scripture, our Catholic teaching, and the sacraments. All of these things mediate our encounter with the Risen Lord and make him present in our lives. On the other hand, Thomas, "the doubter," was asked to believe in Christ's Resurrection on the basis of the witness and the testimony of scared disciples locked in a room. He was not at the empty tomb. Christ had not appeared to him. His unfortunate subtitle has followed him for a long time although it is found nowhere in Scripture. If Thomas is the doubter, it's curious that we find all of the other disciples huddled together in this room. Jesus had already appeared to them, yet one week later they are *again* gathered behind locked doors. One week later! Is it fair to say that only Thomas was puzzled by this Resurrection event? Perhaps Thomas' initial questions arise within him because he hears that the other disciples have already seen the Risen Lord, they've seen his wounds, they're sent forth with his Holy Spirit and commissioned to bring the world mercy, and yet there they are, one week later, still locked in a room.

Thomas says he cannot come to full belief unless he sees the nail marks for himself (like all the others) and unless he touches Jesus. Thomas wasn't completely sure about this awesome event, and I wonder if he was not alone. The other disciples had seen the wounds already, yet they didn't know what to do. Did they yearn for or feel they needed another encounter with the Lord to see his glory again? To have hope fully restored and their fears taken away? Is that so wrong to want? After all, a dead person does not rise. The sight of the Risen Lord most certainly changes the disciples forever, but doesn't it make sense to desire more? Perhaps Thomas articulates those desires for the group—the desire for confidence in Lord, the desire to fulfill Christ's call to share in his mission of love and mercy, the desire to leave the safety and comfort of the locked room, the desire to believe and know with confidence that Jesus is alive.

Despite all of our previous encounters with Christ, despite the years that we have known and experienced him, don't we all find ourselves desiring that something more: more confidence, more security, more faith, more time? Thomas had this same desire. We return time after time to the Eucharist, to take Jesus' Body and Blood into our very selves. Thomas desired to touch Jesus in order to really experience him. He desired to really understand what had happened. He desired to know once and for all that Jesus was everything he said he was.

The desire of Thomas is not doubt, but is love trying to happen. Jesus, as he walks through the locked door of fear, graces the disciples with peace and invites Thomas to touch him. He teaches his disciples that desire is not an emptiness needing to be filled; desire is a fullness needing to be in relationship. Despite the checklist of things that Thomas desires to see and touch in order to believe, Thomas does not reach out and touch Jesus. He doesn't need to. Thomas instead names Jesus. The reality, strength, and confidence of his relationship with Jesus compels

Thomas to name the Risen Christ Lord and God. This intimate and peaceful encounter with Jesus renews the love that had been covered by Thomas' grief and fear. His relationship, and that of all the other disciples, is restored. As much as Thomas "needed" to touch Jesus for himself, he never does. Thomas got much more than his wish to touch Jesus' wounds when he was given the gift of everlasting life—namely, the knowledge that his deepest desires and longings are not for information and facts, but to be in relationship with God. Jesus does not call Thomas "the doubter," just as he does not call Peter "the denier" (for example, see Mark 14:66–72), or any of the other Apostles "deserters" (for example, see Matthew 26:55–56). Satan calls us by our sin. God calls us by name, and gives us the gift of ourselves, our worth in his eyes, and his endless fount of mercy.

Don't we all, like Thomas, desire that "something more"? Have you ever caught yourself asking for a sign from God? For a deeper sense of God's presence? Many people think that's doubt. Could that be, instead, our deepest desire, our love trying to happen through an encounter with Christ?

Conclusion

We work to eliminate sin from our lives and orient our choices and worship to God alone so that we can better hear the voice of the Lord. God is always present, knocking on the doors of our hearts and preparing us to leave the comfort and fear of the upper room in which we are huddled. We reach out to God and affirm our belief. We are animated by his Spirit to new life and boldly go forth in holiness to teach all nations the Good News. This is not merely a Lenten endeavor; rather, it is the work of a lifetime. Lent, as a season of preparation, calls us to look forward to the upcoming joy of Easter. As Christians, we regard our entire life as a preparation for the time of Christ's final triumph, when he comes again and we are taken into the eternal joy and happiness of God's heavenly Kingdom.

Of course, any lifelong commitment is a commitment that is chosen not just once but each and every day. With the help that God's grace provides, we can respond generously to the Lord's call to holiness. It is never too late examine our lives and to accept his gift of love. It is never too late to follow him.

At each and every Mass, we sign ourselves with holy water and recall the saving work of Christ and our adoption by Baptism. We are reminded not just of the act of our Baptism but of our identity in Christ. In the Penitential Act, we recall his mercy and forgiveness to those who cry out to him. We learn the way of Christ through our attentive listening as the Word of God is proclaimed and made present in our midst. We recall his faithfulness throughout salvation history. In the Eucharist, we are transformed to more closely resemble the one whom we receive. We are strengthened in our communion and are given a pledge of life eternal. Changed by this encounter with the crucified and Risen Lord, we are sent out to be a witness of him so that others may encounter Christ and come to recognize their desire for a relationship with God. The pattern of our worship on Sunday, the day of Resurrection, mimics our movement from Lent to Easter. We are called to conversion and to respond to and grow in the grace of our Baptism.

This is why we celebrate Lent and model our lives on that movement of turning away from sin and toward God: to make space within the wounds of our hearts and be moved by so great a desire so as to find God present there.

There is no failure the Lord's love cannot reverse, no humiliation He cannot exchange for blessing, no anger He cannot dissolve, no routine He cannot transfigure. All is swallowed up in victory. He has nothing but gifts to offer. It remains only for us to find how even the cross can be borne as a gift.

—Constitution 8: The Cross, Our Hope
Constitutions of the Congregation of Holy Cross